What Does Anyone Know About Goddesses?

What Does Anyone Know About Goddesses?

Poems by

Gina Malone

© 2025 Gina Malone. All rights reserved.
This material may not be reproduced in any form, published,
reprinted, recorded, performed, broadcast,
rewritten or redistributed without
the explicit permission of Gina Malone.
All such actions are strictly prohibited by law.

Cover design by Shay Culligan
Cover image Terracotta head of a woman; Greek, Tarentine;
late 4th century BCE; Metropolitan Museum of Art, New York;
Gift of Mary and Michael Jaharis, in honor of Thomas P.
Campbell, 2013
Author photo by Juls Buckman

ISBN: 978-1-63980-835-9

Kelsay Books
502 South 1040 East, A-119
American Fork, Utah 84003
Kelsaybooks.com

For my mother, Greer Delores Prevatte, whose voice came to me recently saying, *Don't forget me.* She introduced me to the love of language, she never realized how strong she was, and she taught everyone who ever knew her how to love and how to find their way home.

and

for Richard Baker, the brilliant artist who sat playing guitar on a small-town street in springtime, stole my heart and offered his in return, then challenged me to get out of my own way and *write.*

Acknowledgments

Thank you to the following publications, in which versions of these poems previously appeared.

North Carolina Literary Review: "1970"

Poetry South: "Beginning Again"

Contents

She of the Hearth	11
Another Life Ago	12
Hestia Watches Her Story	14
Arrivals and Departures	16
What Does Anyone Know About Goddesses?	20
After Adrienne Rich (and Before Gloria Steinem)	22
1970	26
Unsung	31
Making a Face	33
A Spirit, Yet a Woman, Too	34
Diary of a Goddess, an Excerpt	36
Bless Me, Father	38
Beginning Again	42
Domesticity	44
Hestia Wakes	45
Contagious Magic	46
The Turkey Baster	48
She Filled Her Home	50
Essence	51
Doing	54
We Are All Goddesses	56

She of the Hearth

In solitude she feeds flames with the fat
of sacrifice, sweeps the stones of ash,
arranges chairs around warmth,
      peeks at bread baking,

sews most evenings, an overflowing
workbasket by her side. She must keep
hands busy,   between times rising
to tend the fire, to poke at and reposition logs, to keep alive
      its burning, burning, ever burning.
            The hearth must not be forsaken.
            Neither the earth. Nor the heart.

As clenched needle works close stitches at veil's edge,
she reflects on that dim time between births,
      the startle of having been
and then not being,

            years when, imprisoned, she waited
to know anew warmth, light, purpose. She frowns,

but when, once more, contentment settles within, she sends
laughter into rooms warmed by other fires, and mortals,
never guessing they are beholden, say how in winter
      a crackling fire comforts.

By the time they think of tea, already
Hestia has slipped from the room to fill a kettle.

Another Life Ago

That first time back, her aunt came down the steps, made of her thin arms a vestibule wide enough that they could all step inside, smiled, and said, *It feels like a lifetime since I saw y'all last.*

But the house, didn't it stare back a little miffed? They had, after all, forsaken it, gone so far away she could not come by and breathe through her nose its sweet must, sit on worn floorboards and plunder reverently the camelback trunks and corner secretary and when through, tuck ledgers and souvenirs, photographs, greeting cards, and letters back where they had always been, it seemed would always be.

Her own letters she found, tied already with ribbon, reading like the yearnings they were. Careful words that beseeched and strutted and lied: *Dear Aunt Cleo, We are fine. Wish you could come visit. You would like it here.*

If only they had never left what was flat, straight, honest, miles of fields and roads, for the sly hills and curves of the piedmont where it's so easy for despair to hide. If only her mother had never chanced upon such a man and moved their lives two hundred miles to his cheap-built house whose walls reverberated with drunken hatred for ready-made daughters. *If only, Mother . . . God, I would be so good, if only . . .* How powerless, children. How impotent, *if only.*

When they left, her mother drove her car. They rode with new coloring books and crayons, and their dolls, rode behind his truck piled with an embarrassment of their belongings tied down tight.

Her sister slept, but she cried for one hundred fifty miles into Betty Sue's dress, then watched the road spool out like rickrack ahead of the car, dipping, then coming up again, held Betty Sue up so she, too, could see how sometimes the truck, to her delight, disappeared, then, to her distress, rose again, could see how the pavement rolled and rolled and rolled—*See the mountains?* her mother had broken the silence with. And *aren't they pretty?* And they were, she nodded, but did not say she would have turned her back on them forever for the horizons of home, for the tree hollow where she left crumbs for fairies, even for the branch that sounded her name nights when it scraped the windowpane.

Years older, she drove long miles back to that old homeplace, bereft by then of anyone who might have welcomed her. Downtown houses looked like faces that had only just stopped crying. They shrank back into overhanging trees and unpruned bushes. Main Street's buildings had drawn shabbiness up around themselves like thin bathrobes, as if they hadn't known this was the day company was coming. It all felt almost, the way dreams will tiptoe around awareness and hide in shadows, slipping away from words that reach for them.

This place doesn't know you, her mind taunted, then whispered, *If only you had never left.*

Hestia Watches Her Story

Hestia stirs ashes and embers, adds another log, then
sits with *Days of Our Lives,* not above needing, wanting,
to watch the lives of others play out in small melodramas
day after day, ludicrous but not impossible the situations
humans get themselves into for the sake of love, lust,
because of vanity, greed, selfishness, dishonesty,

their sins not the worst a person might commit
excepting, of course, the occasional rape or murder.
Anyway, none of it is real when she needs it not to be
and any of it could be when life as a goddess pales
in comparison, her life anyway. The other Olympians
crowd their hours with such longings, jealousies, betrayals,
crimes of passion, always young, always restless,
that they would never sit still for this relative
tameness of human misbehavior.

Like sands through the hourglass,
a disembodied voice intones and yet
the stories employ immortality quite boldly
and in a way that mystifies her,
the Moirai nothing to these mortals.
Why, one man—or is he a demi-god?—
has come back from the dead at least three times.

When a day's episode ends with orchestral lament,
she imagines Bo and Hope and the rest of humankind
somewhere going about their business, monkey
business, while she leans close
to warmth, light, stares into the flames
of a fire that must burn forever, thinks how
between the breadths of future and past lies
the narrow lane of now.

Arrivals and Departures

I.

The honking, distant, grows louder, signal
of intent, and now my eyes
pick them out, the pair, dark-moving against the sky,
watch   as they circle
       glide from on high,
tilt wings at their runway of corn stover, winter
weeds and buttercup.
Like small, fraught planes they land, wings back
and flapping, feet splayed forward
skidding into the wind
                         onto the field.
Morning after morning they arrive.

We who live quiet lives
anticipate, keep timetables
in our heads, clear space
in our days,
       position ourselves for arrivals.

II.

What the dead leave behind we discover—
I find letters, handwritten, overflowing
with such sincerity, somehow formal and
familiar both, telling in plain prose
the most mundane things that years later
fill an outsider with longing.　　　I wish,
for instance, I might sit unseen on the porch
beside the young woman not yet my mother
while she writes to the young man not yet my father,
complains that she has nowhere to be—
inside she will only argue with her sister;
outside, mosquitoes bite and bullfrogs bellow.

I move ideas and make room in memory
for these strangers who remind me of themselves,
so anxious, imperfect, and well-meaning, convincing
themselves with each looping letter
of every heart-shy word that here, at last,
　　　　　　is love.

There he sits clean after second-shift millwork
by a lamp, late, left hand hovering
above the page so as not to smudge the ink—
Send your senior picture when you get it, he will write
in letter after letter, and I know that he wants
to hand-color its grey tones, put in the green
of her dress and eyes, the red of her hair, the glow
of her skin, the white and pink of her smile.
I see her, in literature class, hoping Mr. Prince, *who's trying*,
she writes, *to read poetry aloud,* thinks she is taking notes.

She will tie, with a piece of lace, significance unknown,
the envelopes, tuck them into the trunk where she keeps
every testament to, each artifact of, all the evidence for—love
—where, little by little, they are buried by the years.

III.

Now the geese, running for take-off, call
biddings to one another, and I hardly know how
admiration of them lapsed into meditation on the two
who preceded my being, loved, then did not, stayed together,
then tore apart, recalled grievances, then re-forgot, aged
separately through the years, settled,
when the grandchildren came, into a lull of forbearance.

Suffering, weak near the end, unable to stand
and almost falling out of my arms
my mother once called for him, for his help (*Jimmy!*)
him dead nearly three years by then (*We need you!*)
gone from her life more than thirty.
Those few thousand words were the genesis of
them, us, now. If either
had failed just once to reply—

Mornings, I watch at the window and their quiet
lives, their passions, flow in me still, mingle with mine
so that who knows which of us admires
more the geese, how they mate
for life, have flown apart from the flock to find
their nesting place, how they land and feed,
how their honks fade
down the valley,
how, when they are gone, what's left
              is silence.

What Does Anyone Know About Goddesses?

Hestia runs a finger along spines:
Making a Home; and *Domestic Duties, or,*
Instructions to young married ladies; and this
one, *The Young Housewife's Counsellor and Friend.*
No one would guess she values such compiled advice.
They think she was disgorged complete
with knowledge of how to create and keep,
an innate wisdom of the art, the science, of domesticity.

It serves their narrative to think she never
craves anything else, content to stay
home, mistress of neat, dame of orderly.
She's agoraphobic, they whisper,
shy, a homebody. It's no wonder
she never married. It's just as well.
And if she were married and mortal,
they would say, *it's a woman's place,*
women by nature like their nests.
She hears them, and smiles to herself,
will not let anger rise within. Let them
think what they will. It matters not to her.

She sits keeper of the secret—that all good
homemakers build nests they thrill
to come home to after roaming alone
the dark wilds on moonlit nights.

After Adrienne Rich
(and Before Gloria Steinem)

She had never thought the garage apartment would keep itself;
that was her job, what she wanted to do, could do, did well.
No dust upon the beauty shop furniture of love.
Cheap things—mirrors, vanities with drawers,
vinyl chairs, a laminate table that must have displayed
Ladies Home Journals—all of it came with the place.
Ms. Martha, she said they could call her, everyone did,
had closed her salon and arranged its furnishings here
and seemed proud when she showed them the rooms,
kept complimenting, too, her pretty red hair
and apologized but said she would have to see
the marriage certificate. *Y'all look so young, you know.*
She laughed.

They were not living, had never lived,
in sin. She was eighteen, Class of '65, graduated
in May, married in September, and this place
sheltered their lives, the rooms hers for the time
being to arrange, to tend, to move about in, radio playing,
while he worked for the bag company blocks away, hours every
    day.

At 1:30, she would stop listening to demons,
set down cloth and broom, sit with sandwich and Coca-Cola
and watch *As the World Turns* on the little black-and-white set.
Lisa has left Oakdale for someplace else
and she misses her; she would watch the new

show where she is Lisa still, but it airs
evenings and how strange it would be
to watch her story with him home.
He would laugh and make fun, yawn
probably, want the westerns;
no man could understand the stories, how
young wives, housewives, widows, women
alone with their homes and their yearnings,
needed those doses of drama, of familiarity, of hope.

By evening, she is back in love with this life again.
He comes home tired, showers, and smelling of Palmolive
sits across from her at the table, and she smiles when
he says how good the pork chops taste and looks forward
to when dishes are done and she will lie in bed with his warmth
and the tobacco smell of him   and fall to sleep
thinking how the earth turns and turns.

She will wake sometimes
with earliest daylight peering around the edges
of window shades and straight through the sheer curtains
and know with a nervous flutter that another day in this life
she has chosen will begin soon, with his lunch wrapped
and bagged, a kiss goodbye, and the silence of home
hers again for long hours.

Mothercraft

Her hands create the magic. I crane to see
until she lifts me onto the counter where I perch
in high delight, can watch her rubbing fat and flour
between her fingertips, letting pieces fall, picking up more,
working inside the red bowl with its milk-white interior.

I am four and Mama makes biscuits,
the kitchen window streaked with rain,
makes biscuits while my night-working father
still sleeps. And my toddler sister and baby brother
nap.   My mother never sleeps. She is up
before we are, awake past when we go to bed.
Never dozes or looks heavy-eyed even. There's too much to do.
Always. *You can sleep in the grave*, I remember her saying. But
    not yet,
not until I am old enough to say such things to.

Now she pours in buttermilk and stirs with a fork
while the radio atop the refrigerator plays *Mr. Bojangles*
and, loving the sound, the words, I ask to be let down,
I leave her and the bowl and go stand where
I can look up while I listen.
And, *what does it mean,* I ask?
Where is Mr. Bojangles, whose name sounds
like merriment? And Mama says he is in jail
and I have to know why. *Because he's bad to take a drink,*
she tells me, and I don't know what any of it means,

but I pretend I do, afraid someone
will think I am as stupid as I often feel.

I want to be as wise as they are, knowing what
needs doing always. I want to make biscuits,
too, and Mama gives me a pinch of dough,
asks me to go wake Daddy.
And I do, I climb up on the bed in the room
darkened against day, stand on my knees
and shake his shoulder. When, *I'm awake,*
he says, I jump down, go to my hiding place
and eat the little unbaked biscuit
I have patted round in my hands and believe
that, magical, it has given me all the wisdom they have.
And I decide that I like it here in this clean
house, everything just so, that I'll never be bad
to take a drink and have to dance like Mr. Bojangles
across a cell, but stay until I'm old
enough that Mama and Daddy are the children
and I'm the one to put biscuits in the hot
oven and call them both to supper.

1970

> An original hobby is emerging as the birth of
> a young village near F_____. The new town is
> to be called _____, and Dr. _____ L. _____
> is the owner and originator. (1959)

A minute's worth of memory
of the womanless gloom of a house
that knew me no more than I knew it
is all there is—
my wanting to put fingers on piano keys
despite the dust years-dark upon them,
to hear what music might come out—
my grandmother shaking her head—
clinical sternness in her face—
No.
I was not yet five.

I would be grown before I knew
that it was the faded-grand home of a failed man
she had worked for once as a nurse. We waited
for the end of a beginning too close
on the heels
of my baby brother's birth.

> ... charges and Accusations which were as follows:
> 1. That your mental condition renders you unable
> safely to practice medicine ...

I am glad that I have it, this sliver of then,
a memory, as if it matters, to stave off oblivion.
In my middle years, if I let myself be,

I am beset with unknowing for a life
that might have been entwined with mine.

I could drive myself mad
if I pined, if
I manufactured mourning—
belatedly—for what never was
blanketed and held.

My mother does not know I grieve
for then, for now,
for her, she
who has to have memories,
questions, regrets maybe,
but moreover a bed-made sense of
having done what she had decided
must be done.
I do not ask her anything. I cannot now.
I said little the time thirty years
ago when she did talk of it.
She was cleaning out the closet
of her mind. A discarding.
Here's this sadness, her voice said,
that I have not worn for years.
What words
could I summon then,
with the knowing come suddenly
upon me, a startling,
form separating from shadow?

How unfairly I hate a little
my grandmother, dead now,
for frowning when I only wanted
to bring sound into that stillness,
for babysitting our unawareness,
for taking us all there that day.
And my father?
I will never know what
he said, what he thought.
There are holes in my memory
where he ought to be.

> Dr. _____ was paged in the hotel to which page there was no answer. Mr. Anderson, Attorney, advised that Mr. N. L. Britt, Attorney for Dr. _____ had acknowledged to him that Dr. _____ received notice of the hearing to be held at this time.

He was ever one, my father was, for leaving
all of our lives up to my mother, subordination
having become habit with him.

> ... that the license of Dr. _____ be revoked. Duly seconded. Passed unanimously. (1969)

I don't remember my mother that day.
I pretend her pale and quiet emerging
from that dismal place being
slow-danced to the car, a crumpled partner

in my father's arms.
I know now that she was sick in the days after
with an infection that might have killed her,
but, young, strong, nursed by my grandmother,
she recovered to mother her three.

> There are many known and obvious facts in
> the realm of common knowledge which speak
> for themselves, sometimes even louder
> than witnesses, expert or otherwise.
> The case as made survives the demurrer.
> Reversed.

Once we had stepped out of the draperied dusk
and the fettering wordlessness,
into sunshine and rain-washed freshness
   that I do not actually recall,
into bright birdsong in dull winter
   that I have added for effect to my memory,
into that town two hundred seventeen
miles from home, the place
of my mother's girlhood,
we never went there again
and I could not find my way there now.

Nor can I find his manmade town with its

> three fishing lakes ... and many species of fowl,
> chickens, bantams, pheasants, turkeys, native
> geese, Canadian geese, ducks, guineas and tame
> partridges

on any map.

In my mind, often without meaning to,
I, like a timid apparition, haunt myself
in that dim place barely remembered,
see again the unplayed ivory,
feel the unfamiliarity
and hear the silence that was possibility
passing from this world.

Unsung

Sometimes she   exploded

at the way life was, one day
happening fast on the heels of another,
no one unselfish enough to ask *how
can I help?* mannerly enough to thank her
for singlehandedly minding it all, making
a home for them where they could rest, a place
they could journey back to and be welcomed
and fed, kept warm and dry and safe in,
all of the comforts arising from her working hands, never
still, so much resolve in those strong, long-fingered hands.

*Nobody appreciates a thing I do.
I'm taken for granted. I should never
have got married, never have had children.*
Sighs, tears at times, her frustration
floating with disturbed dust, the broom strokes quick
and violent. Sometimes she rattled pans
to wake them from their long slumbers.

And then, evening would come,
the house, spotless, glowed in lamplight,
they said something sweet
or, shy, brought her a fist of wildflowers

and she forgot her vexation.
Forgiving them, she held out her arms,
and they stepped into the shelter of her.
Her hands drew them in close.

Making a Face

She rubs with firm fingers
foundation along zygomatic arch, into cheek
hollows, carefully around lacrimal and glabella bones,
the practiced hand a woman uses
when she has touched soft skin and the hard structure
beneath it these many years: with wonder or despair,
with familiarity, with acceptance. The way, knowing
and searching both, a mother will touch her child.

Eyes widen, mouth clenches, lips tuck themselves away.
She blends along mandibles, bending her head
back, conceals the demarcation line underneath
her jaw, turns from side to side, dabs
now with a tissue, dusts finally with powder.

Lashes raked, eyebrows darkened, lips traced and shaded,
she smiles, a flash
like lightning, then stares

somber.

A Spirit, Yet a Woman, Too

They assume She wears the veil out of modesty, to signify
She is bride only unto Herself and Her home, a virgin Goddess.
Mortals call women who have not married *maiden
ladies, old maids, spinsters,* and worse, as if they are pitiable
creatures whom time and omission have worn to wraiths.

Hestia laughs at the secret between those untethered
women and Herself. Just as She has, they have prevailed.
They, too, are goddesses, having
chosen for themselves time, autonomy, responsibility
for no one's happiness but their own, solitude, the refuge
of walls, floor and roof, and fire to sit by, meditating,
a home for themselves and not a place
they must keep for others.

Not that She scoffs at marriage and motherhood,
both the most noble of undertakings, crucial, the hardest,
the most thankless, often. When She sees a mortal
sink with despair upon her kitchen floor, Hestia soothes
her brow with a breeze from the window,
lowers the flame of stove or oven, breathes with her
until she feels strong enough to stand and start all over again.

What is living anyway but starting over again every minute
of every day, whether that life is eternal as with Her, or whether
days number much fewer than the hairs on a weary head?

This thought, Hestia guides the harried woman toward.
She bids her make a place of comfort for herself first,
a harbor for her own heart, a setting for rest, reflection,
artistry, for all women are Creators.

Hestia's veil keeps Her long red hair from flames' reach.
That is all. She laughs at how they think they know Her,
how they think they know the heart of any Woman.

Diary of a Goddess, an Excerpt

How then can one describe you [goddess], who keep and hold within yourself the god-sent fire, a remnant of the harmony [of the universe]?
~ Claudia Trophime, 1st c. CE

Divinity of earth, named chief of goddesses, I am
nevertheless shy, deriving my pleasure from seeing others
make merry, having them—happy—offer libations in my name.
They keep home fires burning, as they like to say, and thus
I am always there, though they may forget and attribute
their fire's voice to moisture, to the release of steam
as wood fractures under flame, but it is only I, laughing
with delight at comfort. What a beautiful word *comfort*,
is it not? Warmth, wanting for nothing, tables of sustenance,
walls for well-being, enclosure of love, place of sanctuary.

Why, can you believe some have felt sorry, thought me lonely
among goddesses, branded me a virgin (as if that were a bad thing
    to be)
and a homebody (as if that, too, were a bad thing),
whispered that I was the one who chose chair over throne?

Remember this: love and joy reside in order,
in domesticity, in rituals, in creation of place.
Know that, far from being in my home alone, I dwell
in every home, from the humblest room to the grandest palace.

Wherever someone sighs, says *this is my home,* or *I am home,*
there I abide also. Offerings have ever been the way, but
I say keep a home and keep it well as a refuge for all,
a conservatory for love and peace, a fortress
for the very soul of being.
Then will you pay homage to me.

Bless Me, Father

Bless me, Father, for I have sinned.
And anyway I am not Catholic. These are the only
words I know to preface a confession.
What should I say? I don't go to church anymore.
Most of the time I think I am a witch. I even
bought a book of spells, but a terrible pall came
upon the house when I tried to summon prosperity
and so it must be that I still believe in/fear God/good.

Bless me, Mother, for I have sinned,
and will go on sinning while I search for happiness.
It began with such hope. Well, no, I think I knew all along
that I was marrying to get out of the house, away from
your drunken, hate-filled husband. And when he drove
off White Oak Mountain and died
while I was carrying my first, I don't know
why I cried. Maybe for your sake. Maybe because, vessel for life,
I was sensitive to its fleetingness. Maybe out of relief.
A few years later when my natural father died—nothing.
Not one tear for him who never cared, not even enough to hate me.

Bless me, Spirit, for I have sinned.
I meant for this to go better. I am confessing
the wrong sins, or rather the parts of my life
that are not sins, just steeped in unhappiness,
the parts I wish could have turned out better.
I love my children though, Spirit, love them deeply.
I call them my angels. Three of them. There might have

been a fourth. That may have been a sin, but I could not bear
the thought of being sick again all those months and having
to care for my three stairsteps, the youngest ten months old
and, anyway, Jimmy kept getting laid off
at the mill. But I think of it at times.
What would it have been?
I can't do that. It has to stay a mass of cells
that slipped away. A possibility that became impossible.
You can't humanize it. Well, you do, I'm sure.
God may. I hope She understands.

Bless me, Father, for I have sinned.
When you're eighteen, were you ever eighteen, Father?
Silly—of course you were. But I mean, did you ever feel
that yearning for the best life and not know how to find it?
And just fall into step—get married, get pregnant, keep
house, get pregnant again, keep house, get pregnant again
and everything has to be neat and clean all the time?
Sheets washed and dried on the line, beds made, floors
mopped, rugs shook out, tubs and sinks scrubbed, furniture
dusted—everything in order. And the yard too. Grass mown,
hedges trimmed, porches swept. And everyone must be fed.
And hair and fingernails trimmed, and bodies bathed.
And bills must get paid. And plans made. I never stopped
long enough to be tired.

Bless me, Goddesses, for I have sinned.

There was never enough time for me and so I lost
myself and when another man came along and saw
what I thought had become invisible, I grew infatuated
and kept secrets until Jimmy read my diary
      and knew

           and every—
      thing
                      shattered.
I have heard of a kind of Japanese pottery whose name
I can never remember where broken pieces are put back
together with gold and made beautiful and that's how
I felt, forty years old and lovely again in my own apartment
in another state, children almost grown, thriving
and loving me still.   It was all I needed.

If love, Divine Spirit, gets a person into heaven, into whatever
afterlife there is, and kindness, I have tried to nurture
those things. I never stopped caring, always
tried to make welcoming places for them to come home
to, bring their love and sit with me, drinking tea.
No one ever left empty-handed. And smiles, laughter,
hugs, cards with sweet words of love, ones they would
have been too shy to say aloud. Their offerings to me.

Now that I think of it, never mind the blessings of shadowy
others, of dogmatic patriarchy; atonement for me
will not require counting beads or falling
upon my knees or telling
my secrets to strange men.
My life, I realize, from birth to now
has been blessed, has been the best I could make it.
I'll be leaving now. I thank you for your time.

Beginning Again

She could not recall
ever having ironed
while angry before,
   but how cathartic

to push hot metal hard
   against the soft cotton shirt
   with its pretty pattern,
   clusters of muted cherries;

to be startled
   by the metallic groaning
   of the ironing board
   as it gave way beneath her resolve,
   then straightened itself again;

to hear the sigh of steam escaping,
   echoing her own deep-dredged
   breaths of ragged frustration;
     and how satisfying

to solve the only problem
   the cloth had—wrinkles
   after a washing;

to know she would get over
   the stomach-sunken despair as soon
   as the shirt was smooth
   and his hand was touching
   the still-warm fabric at her back
   as they walked out into the world
   to begin again,

while the iron,
   unplugged,
   cooled in the quiet room.

Domesticity

*There are practical little things in housekeeping
which no man understands.*
       ~Eleanor Roosevelt

She has gone.
He does not have to tell this to the neighbors.
The plants in pots on the back porch
  and on the windowsills
  are dried brown stalks.
He does not see them anymore,
  any more than he ever saw her
  water and care for them.
The dust-dull blinds at the front window
  are crooked, and the WELCOME mat at the door.

She took with her
  things he did not know
  he would miss.
He lives haunted
  and the apartment won't keep
  itself as it did when she slept
  and waked by his side.
The air has gone stale, the light, dim.

She took one suitcase, the mantel clock,
  that painting of Paris, and herself, and left
  emptiness.

Hestia Wakes

like a quiet birth into her surroundings, lies
in ease and lets her eyes adjust to the light, take in
paintings, the chair by the window, a shelf of books,
the glass and porcelain upon her dresser, the rug
her feet will fall upon as she swings legs over bed's edge
to walk from here to hearth.
Dreams disturb with their lack
of order, their incongruity, the nonsense
her slumbering mind takes for true. Even now
her heart quickens at last night's lioness sprawled in the doorway.

Sleep, she has decided, is only to be borne, not
to be relished. For her, the tasks of day, the tending
of fire, the soothing of souls and mending of rifts.
Whenever she sighs the distressed homemaker,
wife, mother, lets go, feels
contentment seep through, slows, and knows
that in time is time enough.
The seconds ticking on the clock seem endless

                        and anyway
haven't goddesses been given all the time in the world?

Contagious Magic

Belongings become leavings,
mundane material objects that outlast their owners
with quiet triumph. They knew it would be so
and curated trifles anyway—
we all do.

Yesterday, chanced upon, the blog
of one who helped dismantle the house
where married laureates had written, lived,
loved, then, years apart—first her, then him—died.
She wrote, this stranger, how paintings
and trinkets, those inconsequentials
that collect dust in corners, now the hushed
and solemn effects of the dead,
lay arranged, priced, and picked over by the living.

(*All destined for the rubbish heap*,
he might have said once, waving his hand
with pencil in it. She might have unbent her gaze
from notebook and nodded, soft-smiled.)

She took home an armload, bemoaning money spent
and more books acquired, but only as an attempt
at humbleness. Don't doubt that she wanted to exult
in what she got, what she could never come near
while they were alive, pieces of the poets, scraps

of their souls, leftover bits of their everyday lives
like the stains in that cold teacup,
string tag hanging from its handle—
his books with scribbled
sticky notes still in place—
a framed rejection letter,
tepid, that she received—
The new owner will hang it close by her own
desk, a reminder that even the great ones
get treated off-handedly by *The New Yorker*.

Sometimes she will run a finger along
the adhering edges of the Post-its protruding
like tongues from pages, imagine
how he must have done the same.

Never so sufficient to us our own existences
that we won't tear like vultures
at the remains of other lives,
the odds and ends the dead
leave behind—always out of place
on our shelves, the way stolen goods
would be—charms, we must think them,
against obscurity.

The Turkey Baster

Looking for long and skinny, cylindrical, flat, anything
that might slip into that narrow space and retrieve
lint from the clothes dryer,

I grabbed her turkey baster, yellow rubber bulb
atop thick plastic tube.　　　　　　It failed—
wrong tool for the job—lay forlorn on the floor
while, ah yes, the vacuum's crevice attachment—

The baster I rinsed and returned to the far back
of the lower cabinet where those kitchen tools
seldom used gather nearly forgotten,
huddled in a corner like refugees.

Such a pointless thing for a vegetarian
to have held on to all this time.
It must be fifty years old, at least, still
in working order as simple things tend to stay.
How would I bring myself to place it in a bag
for the thrift shop or, worse, trash dump?
Who would take it up and remember how it was?
Her hand squeezing the bulb, tube's end
in the glistening juices in the pan,
uncurling her fingers to draw them up,

lifting it tilted like a magic wand, lowering
its tip, positioned, and squeezing again
to release, watching liquid run like a rainstorm
over roasting skin or flesh, yet another way
she was trying to put back what was escaping.

Afterwards, clean and dry, awaiting
the next occasion, the turkey baster lay
at the back of a drawer. It moved with her
from house to house, outlasting
her life, as it's likely to outlast mine.

She Filled Her Home

with mugs and bowls, vases,
baskets, soft cushiony places to sit. There
had to be places to put it, the love, when it overflowed.
She baked it into cookies and squeezed the rinds of it
till juice trickled into fruity teas, always cold,
always in the pitcher waiting to stream
into the empty glass.

When she went, she left it behind, everywhere, in every flowerpot
and mixing bowl, in the cookie jar, in all of the cloth bags
that hang on a nail in the closet. It shines out of light bulbs,
is stored in every drawer, in the filing cabinet, folders of it.

I think of the Swedish, their *döstädning*—
death cleaning—done so that children, heirs, are not left
with all of the belongings.
Such sensible forethought.
Still, I am glad my mother did not know death drew near,
that she did not discard those many receptacles,
but left them
                      filled with the essence of her, air
breathed in and let go of, plans, hopes, wishes,
the dust she never got to wipe away.

Essence

I.

Nineteen years old
tall straight beautiful
gaze bent to newness held fast against your heart.
And whose eye found you there, whose finger lowered
      to fix the moment, separate it from the sand flow

forever, forevermore causing my heart to feel
as flowers must when petals open to a bloom,
so that I breathe deeply against the burgeoning
      to keep myself human?
Was it Daddy?

II.

The night he died, I knocked on your door and
walked into your arms weeping, though you and he
had long since parted ways, and you wept too, and neither of us knew
that within you already rooted, flourishing, was disease.
Our pain you heeded always, and yours we did not perceive.
Forgive us,
please.
Forgive us
for thinking you were, would always be,
strong like a goddess,
invincible, immortal, wise enough to save us all.
What a burden to place upon another, upon a mother.

III.

My friend believes in Biblical heaven, says
that I will see you again, and everyone else who has gone,
that I will not die into darkness as I sometimes imagine.
Funny how I envision others welcomed into the reward
of afterlife, while I
watch from afar.
But then, who can fathom eternity
or space not confined by ground and sky, the great
suspension, no dark and light, no seasons, no fading or failing
of flesh? No flesh even. Or tears.

IV.

I'm listening, you whispered, as we convened
a circle round your bed, pulled the past
into the present and spoke your kindness,
made loud how you loved us, and hoped
you did not hear our grief and feel our tears dampening
the prison you lay within. Those dying, when all other
senses have gone, hear to the last, they say.

V.

That photograph of motherhood I had forgotten—you
proud and glowing and majestic, and me fatly cranky, eyes wincing,
your strong arms and careful hands holding me with wonder—
until you were gone and I sought you in the emptied days.
What love. What pain. Conjoined twins the two, in living as in dying.

Goddesses do not succumb to suffering,
but break free elsewhere
       Radiant.
              Divine.
                     Triumphant.

Doing

Hauntings happen
in the commonplace.   I measure space
across clothesline with dish towel, pin one corner, then the other

and she hovers at my elbow, these the moments
she misses most, what of earthly life she would have again,
not the end-of-day doneness
       but the hourly doing.

If you were ambulatory, what would you like to be doing?
What foolish questions we ask the dying.

My mother's voice stood up out of the pain
that buckled her, caused her to sleep in a chair
hour after hour, day upon day, painkillers
not ruthless enough to assuage her misery:
      I want to clean my house, she said.

The home nurse laughed.
*Clean house? Not walk outside or travel or go
shopping, but clean house?*
Her chuckle nibbled at the silence. Did she hear
one of us say, *She loves her home?*

She wrote who knew what on her forms, useless.
*You can come clean my house too
when you're all well,* she said.

All of the words of solace spoken, times
we told my mother she would be well again.
I believed it even then. Of course
she would be well again, have back
the mundaneness, days when she could take
her health for granted, tackle a list
of Saturday chores or sail off to Ireland.

Oh, I'm glad you're doing that, she would say,
when I dusted, vacuumed, put a vase of flowers
where she could see them, watered the plants.
In the hospice room, hope having
fled, her eyes closed to strange
walls, to our ring of waiting
faces, I dusted, arranged, tidied,
her will resurrected in me. It was
the only way I could let her go.

It's not disconcerting, now, to have her
follow me about while I flick the feather duster,
shovel ashes from the fireplace, make my bed
with breeze-dried sheets.
I like her being here and it's the least I can do, keep
company her spirit, she who
showed us the art, pleasurable,
of making, of keeping, a home, a place
for all the love that outgrows the heart.

We Are All Goddesses

Often an ease steals upon her, and the life of a goddess
being one of relative ease anyway, she shares
this excess with others, with mortals, mostly
women, for they are told you must stay home and
care for house—for husband—for children
and later, now you may go out into the world and work
for it's what you women want, right?
and anyway your earnings, small
as they are, are needed—
      but you must continue to care
           for house—for husband—for children.

Men think they put a woman in her place, when
all the while—Hestia smiles—all the while those women rise,
hour by hour, to take their places alongside her—goddesses too,
      having mastered time and place and man.
      The world swallows women
whereupon they contemplate, imagine, realize, before
they are spat out and find their legs again.

Thereafter, with quiet smiles, they rule the world.

About the Author

When not gazing out the window at her garden, the birds, and the mountains beyond, Gina Malone works as editor of an arts magazine, and writes poetry, fiction, and creative nonfiction.

Awards and recognition include the Sidney Lanier Poetry competition, James Applewhite Poetry contest, and Elizabeth Simpson Smith short story contest. Her work is published in *Kakalak, Poetry South, Streetlight Magazine,* and *Quartet,* among others. At the onset of the COVID shutdown, she set herself the task of writing a poem a day about the pandemic and wrote more than 800 before she was done.

She counts among her greatest life experiences 19 years owning a cozy, secondhand bookstore in the Blue Ridge Mountains where she was able to indulge her love of reading, talk to other booklovers and writers, and still call it a job.

www.ingramcontent.com/pod-product-compliance
Lightning Source LLC
Chambersburg PA
CBHW031205160426
43193CB00008B/518